Hut
DONATION
03/20

D1639744

First published in Great Britain in 1994
This edition first published in 1999 by Dean
an imprint of Egmont Children's Books Limited
239 Kensington High Street, London W8 6SA

Text copyright © 1994 Egmont Children's Books Limited
Illustrations by Arkadia copyright © 1994 Egmont Children's Books Limited
Based on the original television designs by Ivor Wood
copyright © 1994 Woodland Animations Ltd

ISBN 0 603 55985 9

1 3 5 7 9 10 8 6 4 2

A CIP catalogue record for this book is available at the British Library

Printed in Hong Kong

Postman Pat's

Aa

Postman Pat reads the address on every letter.

Miss Hubbard rides her bicycle.

Bb

Cc

Dorothy Thompson gives Pat a cabbage.

Dr Gilbertson is the village doctor.

Dd

Ee

Pat watches the eggs hatch.

Peter Fogg finds a frog.

Ff

Gg

Who forgot to shut the gate?

Jess meets a hedgehog.

Hh

Ii

Ink is messy.

Miss Hubbard makes raspberry jam.

Jj

Kk

Jess keeps away from the dog's kennel.

Pat picks up lots of letters.

Ll

Mm

A magpie has stolen Pat's keys.

Ted Glen has found a birds' nest.

Nn

Oo

Sam Waldron juggles oranges.

Pat delivers a pink parcel.

Pp

Qq

Granny Dryden makes a patchwork quilt.

Reverend Timms grows red roses.

Rr

Ss

Ted Glen buys stamps at the Post Office.

The train goes over the bridge.

Tt

Uu

Pat carries an umbrella when it rains.

Pat looks after his van.

Vv

Ww
Xx

In winter everyone wears extra clothing.

Pat has yellow pyjamas and a duvet with zigzag stripes.

Goodnight, Pat. Sleep well.

Yy
Zz